Start your Cryptocurrency Mining in just 6 hours: for absolute beginners

A. M. Mottaleb

AMM Publishing

ISBN: 978-0-9961593-8-8

CONTENTS

DISCLAIMERS

This book will help you to start learning about cryptocurrency, hands-on with probably under $500, including the price of this book. The ideas, products, or services presented here are not intended to endorse them. They are used in many cases to give practicality of abstract and tough concepts used in the Cryptocurrency world. Therefore, the author uses a very simplistic approach to present complex topics, such as crypto mining. Other books by the author designed for more advanced crypto PoW and PoS are being published. Appendices at the end, after reading the book, you will find excellent resources that can help you with your mining.

This book and any related visual aids (e.g. illustrations, videos, podcasts, etc.) are not intended as technical or financial advice; these materials are intended as an introduction to the world of cryptocurrency mining; you should do further research if you are planning to do it for business, learning, or fun.

INTRODUCTION:
STARTING WITH THE BASICS

Welcome to Cryptocurrency Mining

The book, combined with other resources by the author, is intended to help several types of audiences, or readers; however, mainly this book will benefit two main audiences: first, people who are curious about cryptocurrency; and, second, beginners who want to explore mining, but not sure how. If you are already an avid mining, you probably don't need this book.

Cryptocurrency mining is one of the most exciting and innovative ways to participate in the digital economy. It's the process of validating transactions on a blockchain network and earning rewards in the form of cryptocurrency. While it may sound complex, this book is designed to make it simple, straightforward, and accessible—even for absolute beginners. By the end of this guide, you'll have the knowledge and tools to start your own mining operation in just six hours, or maybe less.

To simplify the concept; a *Blockchain network* is *a decentralized system*, which basically no single entity (e.g. bank or a country, etc.) control. The data is securely stored in linked, chained, blocks. A linked block is linked to digital records in a Blockchain. It offers users transparent, tamper-proof transactions without the need of a central authority, such as a bank or government agencies. This Blockchain process is commonly used for cryptocurrencies and smart contracts.

Why Should You Consider Mining?

1. **Earn Cryptocurrency**: Mining allows you to earn digital currencies like Bitcoin, Ethereum, or Litecoin without having to buy them outright. However, remember that earnings depend on the power of your mining structure. As explained later in this book, producing a currency using less powerful means of mining is almost like winning the lottery!

2. **Support the Blockchain**: Generally, the crypto miners are regular individuals. By mining, you contribute to the security and decentralization of the blockchain network.

3. **Potential for Profit**: Crypto mining is not a get rich quick scheme! Mining requires an initial investment; it can be a profitable venture if done correctly. Again, this book will help you to understand the basics, while you decide if you want to   continue with this journey. The main aim of this book is to make sure what

you should do to start if you decide to get in crypto mining as a venture.

4. **Learn Valuable Skills**: Mining introduces you to the world of blockchain technology, hardware, and software, which are valuable skills in today's tech-driven world. At minimum, you should understand how the cryptocurrency is being made especially that we see that it is gaining momentum and governmental support in USA and around the world.

What is Cryptocurrency Mining?

At its core, cryptocurrency mining involves using computer hardware to solve complex mathematical problems. These problems are part of the process of verifying and adding transactions to the blockchain, a decentralized digital ledger.

[User/ Miner] → [Mining Hardware (e.g. GPU/ASIC)] → [Solving Complex Math Problems]

→[Block Validation] → [Blockchain Network] → [Reward in Cryptocurrency]

Figure one: How Cryptocurrency mining work?

As you see in figure one, the individual user plays an important role, as they select what hardware to buy and invest in. Then, the mining hardware competes to solve these problems, and the first one to succeed is rewarded with cryptocurrency. This process not only secures the network but also introduces new coins into circulation. you don't need math skills to mine cryptocurrency! Math problems are solved by powerful computers, not by people. Miners just need the right hardware (like GPUs or ASICs) and mining software. The computer does all the work automatically.

How It Works (Simplified):

When you look at figure one, it might be a little complicated if you have never done mining before, but, don't worry, it will all make sense later. For now, just remember the process in Figure One is as follows:

1. Miners (mining hardware) take transaction data and combine it with a random number (**nonce**).

2. They run this data through a function, known as the **hash function** (SHA-256 for Bitcoin).

3. The goal is to find a hash that starts with a certain number of **leading zeros** (which makes it very hard to guess).

4. The miner who first finds the correct hash adds the block to the blockchain.

5. If the hash is not found, the miner change the **nonce** and try again—millions of times per second!

Overview of the book and What You'll Learn

This book is your step-by-step guide to starting cryptocurrency mining. Here's what you'll learn:

- The basics of cryptocurrency and how mining works.

- How to choose and set up the right hardware and software.

- How to secure your earnings with cryptocurrency wallets.

- How to start mining and troubleshoot common issues.

- How to stay updated with the latest trends and regulations in the crypto world.

By the end of this book, you'll learn how crypto mining works; more importantly, if you decide that crypto mining is your passion, you can have a fully functional mining operation and the confidence to grow it over time. Again, remember, no one can grantee the success or return-on-investment (ROI). Do your homework before investing big!

Who is This book for?

This book is designed for:

- **Absolute Beginners**: If you've never minded cryptocurrency before, this guide will walk you through every step.

- **Tech Enthusiasts**: If you're curious about blockchain technology and want to get hands-on experience, mining explained here is a great way to start as the book shows practice in easy to follow step-by-step.

- **Investors**: If you're looking to diversify your income streams, mining can be a profitable addition to your portfolio. Again, the ROI depends on the amount of investment, especially that mining attracts many tech savvies; therefore, do more analysis before spending thousands of dollars on mining if you decide to invest big investment.

- **Anyone Interested in Cryptocurrency**: Whether you're a hobbyist or a future crypto expert, this book will give you the tools to learning in a practical manner; then you can decide if crypto mining is for you.

What You'll Achieve in 6 Hours

1.   **Set Up Your First Mining Operation**: From choosing hardware to installing software, to selecting hot/cold wallets; basically, you'll have everything you need to start mining.

2.   **Understand the Basics of Cryptocurrency and Mining**: You'll learn how blockchain technology works and why mining is essential.

3. **Be Ready to Mine and Earn Cryptocurrency**: By the end of this guide, you'll be actively mining.

How to Use This book

This book is structured to guide you through the process of starting your mining operation in a logical, step-by-step manner. Each chapter builds on the previous one, so it's best to follow the order of the chapters. However, if you're already familiar with certain topics, feel free to skip ahead.

A Final Note Before You Begin

Cryptocurrency mining is an exciting journey, but it's important to *approach it with patience and a willingness to learn*. The crypto world is constantly evolving, and staying informed is key to your success. With this book as your guide, you're well on your way to becoming a confident and successful miner.

Let's get started!

Next Chapter Preview: Chapter 1 – Understanding Cryptocurrency & Mining

In the next chapter, we'll dive deeper into the world of cryptocurrency and mining. You'll learn about the history of cryptocurrency, how blockchain technology works, and the role of miners in this world. We'll also explore together the differences between Proof of Work (PoW) and Proof of Stake (PoS) and discuss why mining can be a rewarding endeavor. Be patient; this is building block to your knowledge. You just need maximum one hour per day for six days and you are on your way mining.

Start your Cryptocurrency Mining in just 6 hours

.

CHAPTER 1 - FIRST HOUR
UNDERSTANDING CRYPTOCURRENCY AND MINING

What is Cryptocurrency?

This book and any related visual aids (e.g. illustrations, videos, podcasts, etc.) are not intended as technical or financial advice; these materials are intended as an introduction to the world of cryptocurrency mining; you should do further research if you are planning to do it for business, learning, or fun.

Cryptocurrency is a digital or virtual form of currency that uses cryptography for security. Unlike traditional currencies issued by governments (like the US dollar or Euro), cryptocurrencies operate on decentralized networks based on blockchain technology. This decentralization means no single entity controls the currency, making it resistant to censorship and interference.

- **Brief History of Cryptocurrency**:
  This book is not meant to be an academic; therefore, it will not delve deep into the history of cryptocurrency. The concept of digital currency dates back to the 1980s. However, it wasn't until 2009 that Bitcoin, when the first decentralized cryptocurrency,

was introduced by an anonymous person or group known as Satoshi Nakamoto. Bitcoin's success paved the way for thousands of other cryptocurrencies, including Ethereum, Litecoin, and Ripple.

- **How Cryptocurrencies Work:**
  Cryptocurrencies rely on blockchain technology, a distributed ledger that records all transactions across a network of computers. Each block in the chain contains a list of transactions, and once a block is added, it cannot be altered.

What is Cryptocurrency Mining?

Cryptocurrency mining is the process of validating transactions and adding them to the blockchain. Miners use powerful computers to solve complex mathematical problems, and the first miner to solve the problem gets to add the block to the blockchain and is rewarded with cryptocurrency.

- **The Role of Miners in the Blockchain:**
  Miners play a crucial role in maintaining the integrity and security of the blockchain. They verify transactions, prevent double-spending, and ensure the network remains decentralized.

- **So, you might ask,** so, just clarify when we say miners we mean the hardware (computers, etc.), not people, right?

  The simple answer is when we say **miners**, we usually mean **both** the **people** and the **hardware** they use.

Miners (People)

- ❖ These are individuals or groups who **own and operate** the mining hardware.

- ❖ They set up, maintain, and manage the mining process.

Miners (Hardware) 💻

❖ These are the **computers** (ASICs, GPUs) that actually do the mining work.

❖ They solve cryptographic puzzles and compete to add new blocks.

So, **people (miners) use mining hardware (machines) to mine cryptocurrency**. The hardware does the hard math, but people control and manage it.

- **Proof of Work (PoW) vs. Proof of Stake (PoS)**:

  o **Proof of Work (PoW)**: This is the original consensus mechanism used by Bitcoin and many other cryptocurrencies. Miners compete to solve complex puzzles, and the winner gets to add the block and earn rewards. PoW is energy-intensive but highly secure.

Let's make it simple! Imagine a giant treasure hunt!

There's a huge digital treasure chest (the blockchain), and inside it are shiny gold coins (cryptocurrency). But to open the chest, you need to solve a super tricky riddle. That's where the miners come in!

Miners are like treasure hunters with super-powerful computers. They race against each other to solve the riddle first. The fastest one unlocks the chest, gets some treasure (new coins), and helps keep the treasure map (the blockchain) safe and updated for everyone.

But here's the catch: their tools (computers) use a LOT of energy, like running a million flashlights all day long! That's why some people want a new way to hunt for treasure that doesn't waste so much energy—like Proof of Stake (PoS), where you don't need to solve riddles, just prove you have enough treasure to help protect the chest.

So, miners are digital treasure hunters who work hard, solve puzzles, and keep the system safe—but of course, there will be higher energy cost!

- o **Proof of Stake (PoS)**: In PoS, validators are chosen to create new blocks based on the number of coins they hold and are willing to "stake" as collateral. PoS is more energy-efficient than PoW and is used by cryptocurrencies like Ethereum 2.0.

Sure! Let's imagine a different kind of treasure hunt, but this time, it's **VIP access** instead of a race!

Instead of running around solving riddles like in Proof of Work (PoW), here's how **Proof of Stake (PoS)** works:

Imagine there's a **big treasure vault** (the blockchain), and only trusted guardians are allowed to open it and check that everything inside is fair and correct. But how do we choose these guardians?

Instead of solving puzzles, we pick people who already **own some treasure** (cryptocurrency). The more treasure they have and "lock up" (stake), the higher their chances of being chosen as a guardian. **It's like getting a VIP pass**—if you've got enough treasure, you're trusted to help manage the vault.

These guardians (validators) don't have to use tons of electricity or supercomputers. They just **promise to be honest** by locking up some of their own treasure. If they cheat, they **lose** some of their treasure as punishment! But if they do their job right, they **earn more treasure** over time.

So, instead of a **race** like PoW, **PoS is like becoming a trusted VIP**—where you prove you're responsible by staking your treasure, keeping the system safe, and getting rewarded!

Why Mine Cryptocurrency?

Mining cryptocurrency can be a rewarding endeavor, but it's important to understand both the potential benefits and challenges.

I.   **Potential Benefits: Earnings and Rewards**:
     Mining can be profitable, especially if you mine popular cryptocurrencies like Bitcoin or Ethereum. Miners earn block rewards (newly minted coins) and transaction fees for their efforts.

     1. Passive Income Stream
     - Even on a small scale, mining can generate a steady stream of cryptocurrency, which can be held, traded, or reinvested. However, you should invest carefully.

- While large-scale mining farms dominate, solo miners can still earn some profits, especially with energy-efficient setups.

2. Low Entry Barriers for Certain Cryptos

- While mining Bitcoin (BTC) requires expensive ASIC machines, many **alternative coins (altcoins)** like Ethereum Classic (ETC), Ravencoin (RVN), and Monero (XMR) can be mined using regular **GPUs (graphics cards)**.
- Some newer proof-of-work (PoW) cryptocurrencies have lower difficulty levels, making them accessible to solo miners.

3. Learning and Experimentation

- Mining provides **hands-on experience** with blockchain technology, wallets, mining pools, and crypto transactions.
- It can be a great way to learn about **hardware, software configurations, and decentralized networks**.

4. Utilize older (idle) Powerful systems

- If you already have a powerful gaming PC with a high-end GPU, you can mine when not using it (e.g., overnight).
- This allows you to **monetize existing hardware** without additional investment.

5. Supporting Decentralization

- By mining, you contribute to the decentralization and security of blockchain networks.
- Instead of relying on big mining farms, more individual miners help keep networks distributed.

6. Using Renewable or Low-Cost Energy

- If you have access to **solar power** or lower electricity rates (e.g., off-peak hours), mining can be more cost-effective.

- Some miners repurpose waste heat from their rigs to warm rooms or water, making use of otherwise wasted energy.

- **Potential Risks and Challenges in Crypto Mining**:

  o **High Initial Costs**: Setting up a mining operation can be expensive, especially if you invest in high-end hardware.

  o **Electricity Costs**: Mining consumes a significant amount of electricity, which can eat into your profits.

  o **Market Volatility**: The value of cryptocurrencies can fluctuate dramatically, affecting your earnings.

  o **Technical Knowledge**: Mining requires some technical expertise, though this book will guide you through the process.

Popular Cryptocurrencies to Mine

Not all cryptocurrencies are created equal when it comes to mining. Here are some of the most popular options for beginners:

- **Bitcoin (BTC)**: The first and most well-known cryptocurrency. Bitcoin mining is highly competitive and requires specialized hardware (ASICs).

- **Ethereum (ETH)**: The second-largest cryptocurrency by market cap. Ethereum mining is more accessible to beginners, especially with GPUs.

- **Litecoin (LTC)**: Often referred to as the "silver to Bitcoin's gold," Litecoin is easier to mine than Bitcoin and uses a different mining algorithm (Scrypt).

- **Other Altcoins**: Cryptocurrencies like Monero (XMR), Zcash (ZEC), and Ravencoin (RVN) are also popular among miners due to their lower competition and unique features.

- **Factors to Consider When Choosing a Cryptocurrency to Mine**:

- o **Profitability**: Use online calculators to estimate potential earnings based on your hardware and electricity costs.

- o **Mining Difficulty**: Some cryptocurrencies are easier to mine than others.

- o **Market Trends**: Research the long-term potential of the cryptocurrency you plan to mine.

- o **Hardware Compatibility**: Ensure your hardware is suitable for the cryptocurrency you choose.

Key Takeaways from Chapter 1

- Cryptocurrency is a digital currency that operates on decentralized blockchain technology.

- Mining is the process of validating transactions and adding them to the blockchain.

- Proof of Work (PoW) and Proof of Stake (PoS) are the two main consensus mechanisms used in cryptocurrency.

- Mining can be profitable but comes with risks, including high costs and market volatility.

- Popular cryptocurrencies to mine include Bitcoin, Ethereum, Litecoin, and various altcoins.

Next Chapter Preview: Chapter 2 – Getting Started with Mining Hardware

In the next chapter, we'll dive into the hardware you'll need to start mining. You'll learn about the differences between CPUs, GPUs, and ASICs, explore mini-miners as a beginner-friendly option, and discover how to use a laptop for mining until you're ready to scale up. We'll also cover the basics of building your first mining rig and discuss cloud mining as an alternative.

CHAPTER 2: SECOND HOUR
GETTING STARTED WITH MINING HARDWARE (STEP-BY-STEP GUIDE FOR BEGINNERS)

Learning about Cryptocurrency mining doesn't have to be complicated or expensive. One common story, you will see crypto enthusiasts spending thousands of dollars to learn how to mine; then they lose interest and significant amount of money; this book presenting more affordable to teach you, in only *six-hours* about how mining is done.

In this chapter, we'll walk you through **three beginner-friendly methods** to start mining, starting with the simplest and most affordable option (mini-miners) and progressing to more advanced setups for higher profitability. Each method is explained in a **step-by-step, beginner-proof way**, so you can choose the one that best suits your budget and goals.

Method 1: Mini-Miners – The Easiest Way to Start Mining

Mini-miners are small, affordable devices that plug into your computer or router (physical or wireless). They're perfect for absolute beginners who want to dip their toes into mining without spending a lot of money. Let's use the **NerdMiner V2 Pro (78KH/s Mini Lottery BTC Miner)** as an example.

Step 1: What is the NerdMiner V2 Pro?

- The NerdMiner V2 Pro is a compact, USB-powered device designed for solo Bitcoin mining. It's not designed to make you rich but is a fun and educational way to learn about mining.

- **Hash Rate**: 78 KH/s (very low compared to professional miners, but great device for beginners to learn and explore).

- **Power Consumption**: Extremely low (runs on USB power).

- **Cost**: Affordable (around $50–$100, depending on availability).

Step 2: What You'll Need

1. **NerdMiner V2 Pro**: Purchase the device from a reputable seller.

2. **Computer or Router**: To power and configure the miner.

3. **Internet Connection**: Stable Wi-Fi or Ethernet connection.

4. **Wallet Address**: A Bitcoin wallet to receive your earnings (we'll cover wallets in Chapter 4).

Step 3: Setting Up the NerdMiner V2 Pro

1. **Unbox the Device**: The NerdMiner V2 Pro comes with a USB cable and the miner itself.

2. **Connect to Power**: Plug the USB cable into your computer or a USB power adapter.

3. **Access the Miner's Interface**:

     o The NerdMiner creates its own Wi-Fi network. Connect your computer or phone to this network.

     o Open a web browser and go to the miner's IP address (usually provided in the manual).

4. **Configure the Miner**:

     o Enter your Bitcoin wallet address in the settings.

     o Choose a mining pool (if applicable) or set it to solo mining (default for NerdMiner).

5. **Start Mining**: Click "Start Mining" and watch your device work. You'll see real-time stats like hash rate and temperature.

Step 4: What to Expect

- **Earnings**: The NerdMiner V2 Pro is not designed for high profitability. It's more of a lottery system—you might earn a small amount of Bitcoin if you get lucky.

- **Learning Experience**: This is a great way to understand how mining works without a big investment.

Method 2: Mining with a Laptop – A Slightly More Advanced Option

If you're ready to move beyond mini-miners, you can use your laptop to mine more profitable cryptocurrencies like Monero (XMR). Here's how:

Step 1: What You'll Need

1. **Laptop**: Any modern laptop with a decent CPU (Intel i5 or better).

2. **Mining Software**: We'll use **XMRig** (a popular Monero mining software).

3. **Wallet Address**: A Monero wallet to receive your earnings.

Step 2: Setting Up XMRig

1. **Download XMRig**:

    o Go to the official XMRig website (https://xmrig.com) and download the software for your operating system (Windows, macOS, or Linux).

2. **Configure XMRig**:

    o Extract the downloaded files to a folder on your laptop.

    o Open the config.json file in a text editor.

    o Replace the default wallet address with your Monero wallet address.

    o Save the file.

3. **Start Mining**:

    o Open the folder where you extracted XMRig.

    o Double-click the xmrig.exe file to start mining.

    o You'll see real-time stats like hash rate and earnings.

Step 3: Tips for Laptop Mining

- **Cooling**: Use a cooling pad to prevent overheating.

- **Power Settings**: Set your laptop to "High Performance" mode.

- **Mining Pools**: Join a Monero mining pool (like SupportXMR) to increase your chances of earning rewards.

Step 4: What to Expect

- **Earnings**: Laptop mining is more profitable than mini-miners but still limited. You might earn a few dollars a month, depending on your laptop's performance.

- **Risks**: Mining can strain your laptop and reduce its lifespan, so proceed with caution.

Method 3: Building a Mining Rig – For Higher Profitability

If you're serious about mining and want to earn more, building a mining rig is the way to go. A mining rig is a custom-built computer designed specifically for mining cryptocurrency.

Step 1: What You'll Need

1. **GPUs**: At least 1-2 GPUs (NVIDIA GTX 1660 or AMD RX 580 are good starter options).

2. **Motherboard**: A motherboard with multiple PCIe slots (e.g., ASUS B250 Mining Expert).

3. **Power Supply Unit (PSU)**: A high-wattage PSU (e.g., 750W or higher).

4. **RAM**: 4GB or more.

5. **Storage**: A small SSD (120GB) or USB drive.

6. **Frame**: An open-air frame to keep your components cool.

Step 2: Assembling the Mining Rig

1. **Build the Frame**: Assemble the open-air frame according to the instructions.

2. **Install the Motherboard**: Secure the motherboard to the frame.

3. **Install the CPU and RAM**: Insert the CPU and RAM into the motherboard.

4. **Connect the GPUs**: Insert the GPUs into the PCIe slots and connect them to the power supply.

5. **Install the PSU**: Mount the power supply and connect it to the motherboard and GPUs.

6. **Add Storage**: Connect the SSD or USB drive and install the operating system (e.g., Windows or HiveOS).

Step 3: Setting Up Mining Software

1. **Download Mining Software**: Choose software like **NiceHash** or **PhoenixMiner**.

2. **Configure the Software**: Enter your wallet address and choose a mining pool.

3. **Start Mining**: Launch the software and watch your rig work.

Step 4: What to Expect

- **Earnings**: A mining rig can earn $5–$20 per day, depending on the GPUs and electricity costs.

- **Investment**: Expect to spend $1,000–$10,000 upfront, but the rig can pay for itself over time.

Key Takeaways from Chapter 2

- **Mini-Miners**: Affordable and easy to set up, great for learning (e.g., NerdMiner V2 Pro).

- **Laptop Mining**: Slightly more profitable but limited by hardware capabilities.

- **Mining Rig**: The most profitable option but requires a larger upfront investment.

Next Chapter Preview: Chapter 3 – Setting Up Your Mining Software

In the next chapter, we'll dive into the software side of mining. You'll learn how to choose the right mining software, install and configure it, and join a mining pool to increase your chances of earning rewards. We'll also discuss the differences between solo mining and pool mining.

Start your Cryptocurrency Mining in just 6 hours

.

CHAPTER 3 – THIRD HOUR
CRYPTOCURRENCY WALLETS AND SECURITY

Before you start mining, you need a **cryptocurrency wallet**—a secure place to store, manage, and protect your earnings. This chapter will guide you, step-by-step, through everything you need to know about wallets, from choosing the right type to setting one up and keeping it secure. By the end of this chapter, you'll have a wallet ready to receive your mining rewards.

What is a Cryptocurrency Wallet?

A cryptocurrency wallet is a tool that allows you to store, send, and receive digital currencies. It doesn't actually "store" your coins; instead, it stores your **private keys**—the cryptographic codes that give you access to your funds on the blockchain. Think of it like a keychain that holds the keys to your crypto.

Types of Wallets

There are several types of wallets, each with its own pros and cons. Here's a breakdown:

1. **Hot Wallets:**

   o **What it is**: Wallets connected to the internet.

   o **Examples**: Mobile apps (Trust Wallet, Exodus), desktop apps (Electrum), and web-based wallets (MetaMask).

   o **Pros**: Easy to use, convenient for frequent transactions.

   o **Cons**: Less secure because they're online and vulnerable to hacking.

2. **Cold Wallets:**

   o **What it is**: Wallets not connected to the internet.

   o **Examples**: Hardware wallets (Ledger Nano X, Trezor) and paper wallets.

   o **Pros**: Highly secure, ideal for long-term storage.

   o **Cons**: Less convenient for frequent transactions.

3. **Hardware Wallets:**

   o **What it is**: Physical devices that store your private keys offline.

   o **Examples**: Ledger Nano X, Trezor Model T.

   o **Pros**: Combines security and convenience, supports multiple cryptocurrencies.

   o **Cons**: Costs money (usually $50 – $150).

Choosing the Right Wallet

The wallet you choose depends on your needs. Here's a quick guide:

- **For Beginners**: Start with a hot wallet like **Exodus** or **Trust Wallet**. They're easy to use and great for small amounts.

- **For Long-Term Storage**: Use a hardware wallet like the **Ledger Nano X** or **Trezor**.

- **For Frequent Transactions**: Use a mobile or desktop wallet for convenience.

Setting Up a Wallet (Step-by-Step)

Option 1: Setting Up a Hot Wallet (Exodus)

Exodus is a popular hot wallet that supports multiple cryptocurrencies and is beginner-friendly. Here's how to set it up:

Step 1: Download Exodus

1. Go to the official Exodus website (https://www.exodus.com).

2. Download the version for your operating system (Windows, macOS, or Linux).

Step 2: Install Exodus

1. Open the downloaded file and follow the on-screen instructions to install the software.

2. Once installed, launch Exodus.

Step 3: Create a New Wallet

1. Click "Create a New Wallet."

2. Exodus will generate a 12-word recovery phrase. Write this down on a piece of paper and store it in a safe place.

   o **Important**: Never share your recovery phrase with anyone. It's the only way to recover your funds if your device is lost or damaged.

3. Confirm your recovery phrase by entering the words in the correct order.

Step 4: Start Using Your Wallet

1. Once your wallet is set up, you'll see your dashboard.

2. To receive funds, click on the cryptocurrency you want to receive (e.g., Bitcoin) and click "Receive."

3. Copy the wallet address and share it with your mining pool or software.

Option 2: Setting Up a Hardware Wallet (Ledger Nano X)

The **Ledger Nano X** is one of the most popular hardware wallets, known for its security and ease of use. Here's how to set it up:

Step 1: Unbox Your Ledger Nano X

- Inside the box, you'll find the Ledger Nano X device, a USB cable, a recovery sheet, and a keychain strap.

Step 2: Initialize the Device

1. **Connect to Power**: Plug the USB cable into your computer and the Ledger Nano X.

2. **Turn On the Device**: Press the button on the Ledger to power it on.

3. **Set Up as New Device**: Choose "Set up as new device" on the screen.

Step 3: Write Down Your Recovery Phrase

1. **Recovery Phrase**: The Ledger will display a 24-word recovery phrase. Write this down on the recovery sheet and store it in a safe place.

   o **Important**: Never share your recovery phrase with anyone. It's the only way to recover your funds if your device is lost or damaged.

2. **Confirm the Phrase**: The Ledger will ask you to confirm the recovery phrase by selecting the words in the correct order.

Step 4: Install Ledger Live

1. **Download Ledger Live**: Go to the official Ledger website (https://www.ledger.com) and download Ledger Live for your operating system (Windows, macOS, or Linux).

2. **Install the App**: Follow the on-screen instructions to install Ledger Live.

Step 5: Add Accounts

1. **Open Ledger Live**: Launch the app and connect your Ledger Nano X.

2. **Add Cryptocurrency Accounts**: Click "Add Account" and select the cryptocurrency you want to store (e.g., Bitcoin, Ethereum).

3. **Receive Funds**: Click "Receive" to generate a wallet address. Use this address to transfer your mined cryptocurrency to your Ledger.

Security Best Practices

Keeping your cryptocurrency safe is crucial. Here are some tips:

1. **Protect Your Private Keys**:
   o Never share your private keys or recovery phrase with anyone.
   o Store your recovery phrase offline in a secure location (e.g., a safe).

2. **Use Two-Factor Authentication (2FA)**:

    o   Enable 2FA on all your crypto accounts for an extra layer of security.

3. **Avoid Phishing Scams**:

    o   Be cautious of fake websites and emails pretending to be from legitimate crypto services.

    o   Always double-check URLs and only download software from official sources.

4. **Keep Your Software Updated**:

    o   Regularly update your wallet software and firmware (for hardware wallets) to protect against vulnerabilities.

Why You Need a Wallet Before Mining

Before you start mining, it's important to have a wallet ready because:

- **Mining pools and software require a wallet address** to send your earnings.

- **You need a secure place to store your funds** from the very beginning.

- **Delays in setting up a wallet** could mean delays in receiving your earnings.

Key Takeaways from Chapter 3

- Cryptocurrency wallets store your private keys, not your coins.

- Hot wallets are convenient but less secure, while cold wallets (like the Ledger Nano X) are ideal for long-term storage.

- Setting up a wallet involves downloading the software, writing down your recovery phrase, and generating a wallet address.

- Security best practices include protecting your private keys, using 2FA, and avoiding phishing scams.

- **Set up your wallet before mining** to ensure you have a secure place to store your earnings.

Next Chapter Preview: Chapter 4 – Setting Up Your Mining Software

In the next chapter, we'll dive into the software side of mining. You'll learn how to choose the right mining software, install and configure it, and join a mining pool to increase your chances of earning rewards. We'll also discuss the differences between solo mining and pool mining.

Start your Cryptocurrency Mining in just 6 hours

CHAPTER 4 – FOURTH HOUR
SETTING UP YOUR MINING SOFTWARE

Now that you've set up your **wallet** (Chapter 3) and chosen your **mining hardware** (Chapter 2), it's time to bring everything together with the right **mining software**. Mining software is the tool that connects your hardware to the blockchain network, allowing you to start earning cryptocurrency. In this chapter, we'll walk you through choosing, installing, and configuring mining software, as well as joining a mining pool to maximize your earnings.

What is Mining Software?

Mining software is a program that allows your hardware to communicate with the blockchain network. It performs the complex calculations required for mining and sends the results to the network. The software you choose depends on the **cryptocurrency you're mining** and the **hardware you're using**.

Choosing the Right Mining Software

Here's a breakdown of the most popular mining software options, tailored to the hardware methods discussed in Chapter 2:

1. Mini-Miners (e.g., NerdMiner V2 Pro)

- **Built-In Software**: Most mini-miners, like the NerdMiner V2 Pro, come with their own software interface.

- **What to Do**:

    1. Connect the mini-miner to your computer or router via USB.

    2. Access the miner's web interface by connecting to its Wi-Fi network and entering the IP address in your browser.

    3. Enter your wallet address and start mining.

2. Laptop Mining

- **Recommended Software**:

    o **XMRig** (for Monero and other CPU-mineable coins).

    o **NiceHash** (for multiple coins, beginner-friendly).

- **Steps to Set Up XMRig**:

    1. Download XMRig from the official website (https://xmrig.com).

    2. Extract the files and edit the config.json file to include your wallet address and mining pool details.

    3. Run the xmrig.exe file to start mining.

- **Steps to Set Up NiceHash**:

1. Download NiceHash from the official website (https://www.nicehash.com).

2. Install the software and create an account.

3. Select your laptop's CPU or GPU and click "Start" to begin mining.

3. Mining Rigs (GPU or ASIC)

- **Recommended Software**:

  o **PhoenixMiner** (for Ethereum and other GPU-mineable coins).

  o **CGMiner** (for ASIC miners).

- **Steps to Set Up PhoenixMiner**:

  1. Download PhoenixMiner from the official GitHub page.

  2. Extract the files and edit the start.bat file to include your wallet address and mining pool details.

  3. Run the start.bat file to begin mining.

- **Steps to Set Up CGMiner**:

  1. Download CGMiner from the official website.

  2. Configure the software by entering your mining pool details and wallet address.

  3. Launch CGMiner and monitor your mining stats.

Joining a Mining Pool

Mining pools allow miners to combine their computing power to increase their chances of earning rewards. Here's how to join one:

Step 1: Choose a Mining Pool

- **For Bitcoin**: Use Slush Pool or F2Pool.

- **For Ethereum**: Use Ethermine or SparkPool.

- **For Monero**: Use SupportXMR or MineXMR.

Step 2: Create an Account

- Sign up for an account on the mining pool's website.

Step 3: Configure Your Mining Software

- Open your mining software (e.g., PhoenixMiner, XMRig).

- Enter the pool's server address, your wallet address, and a worker name (optional).

- Save the configuration and start mining.

Step 4: Monitor Your Earnings

- Log in to your mining pool account to track your earnings and payouts.

Solo Mining vs. Pool Mining

- **Solo Mining**:

  - **What it is**: Mining on your own without joining a pool.

  - **Pros**: You keep 100% of the block reward if you solve a block.

  - **Cons**: Extremely low chances of earning rewards, especially for beginners.

- **Pool Mining**:

  - **What it is**: Combining your hash power with other miners to increase your chances of earning rewards.

  - **Pros**: More consistent payouts, even for small miners.

  - **Cons**: You share the block reward with other pool members, and pools charge a small fee (usually 1-2%).

Troubleshooting Common Issues

Even with the right software, you might encounter some issues. Here's how to solve them:

1. **Miner Not Working**:

   - Check your internet connection.

   - Ensure your wallet address and pool settings are correct.

   - Update your mining software to the latest version.

2. **Low Hash Rate**:

   - Make sure your hardware is properly configured.

   - Check for overheating and adjust cooling settings.

   - Update your GPU drivers.

3. **High Rejection Rate**:

   - This means many of your shares are being rejected by the pool.

   - Check your internet latency and try connecting to a pool server closer to your location.

Key Takeaways from Chapter 4

- Mining software connects your hardware to the blockchain network.

- Popular options include **XMRig** (for CPU mining), **NiceHash** (for beginners), **PhoenixMiner** (for GPU mining), and **CGMiner** (for ASICs).

- Joining a mining pool increases your chances of earning rewards.

- Solo mining is less profitable for beginners compared to pool mining.

- Troubleshooting common issues ensures your mining operation runs smoothly.

Next Chapter Preview: Chapter 5 – Mining in Action

In the next chapter, we'll put everything you've learned into practice. You'll learn how to start your first mining operation, monitor your performance, troubleshoot common issues, and calculate your profits. We'll also discuss how to scale up your mining operation for higher earnings.

Start your Cryptocurrency Mining in just 6 hours

CHAPTER 5 - HOUR MINING IN ACTION

Congratulations! By now, you've set up your **wallet** (Chapter 3), chosen your **mining hardware** (Chapter 2), and installed your **mining software** (Chapter 4). In this chapter, we'll put everything into action. You'll learn how to start your first mining operation, monitor your performance, troubleshoot common issues, and calculate your profits. By the end of this chapter, you'll be actively mining and earning cryptocurrency!

Step 1: Starting Your First Mining Operation

1.1 Mini-Miners (e.g., NerdMiner V2 Pro)

If you're using a mini-miner like the NerdMiner V2 Pro, here's how to start mining:

1. **Connect the Mini-Miner**: Plug the NerdMiner into your computer or router using the USB cable.

2. **Access the Web Interface**:

   o Connect to the miner's Wi-Fi network (check the manual for the network name and password).

   o Open a web browser and enter the miner's IP address (e.g., 192.168.4.1).

3. **Enter Your Wallet Address**:

   o In the miner's interface, enter your Bitcoin wallet address (from Chapter 3).

4. **Start Mining**: Click "Start Mining" and watch your device work. You'll see real-time stats like hash rate and temperature.

1.2 Laptop Mining

If you're mining with a laptop, here's how to start:

1. **Launch Your Mining Software**:

   o For **XMRig**: Open the folder where you extracted XMRig and double-click xmrig.exe.

   o For **NiceHash**: Open NiceHash, select your CPU or GPU, and click "Start."

2. **Monitor Your Mining**:

   o Your mining software will display real-time stats like hash rate, earnings, and temperature.

   o If you're using a mining pool, log in to your pool account to track your earnings.

1.3 Mining Rigs

If you've built a mining rig, here's how to start:

1. **Launch Your Mining Software**:

   o For **PhoenixMiner**: Open the folder where you extracted PhoenixMiner and double-click start.bat.

   o For **CGMiner**: Launch CGMiner and monitor your mining stats.

2. **Monitor Your Mining**:

   o Your mining software will display real-time stats like hash rate, accepted shares, and temperature.

   o If you're using a mining pool, log in to your pool account to track your earnings.

Step 2: Monitoring Your Mining Performance

2.1 Key Metrics to Watch

- **Hash Rate**: The speed at which your hardware is solving mining problems. A higher hash rate means better chances of earning rewards.

- **Accepted Shares**: The number of valid solutions your hardware has submitted to the mining pool.

- **Temperature**: The temperature of your hardware. Overheating can damage your equipment, so keep an eye on this.

- **Earnings**: The amount of cryptocurrency you've earned so far.

2.2 Using Mining Software Dashboards

Most mining software and pools provide a dashboard where you can monitor your performance. Here's what to look for:

- **NiceHash**: Open the NiceHash app or log in to your NiceHash account online to view your earnings and hash rate.

- **XMRig**: The command-line interface will display real-time stats like hash rate and accepted shares.

- **Mining Pools**: Log in to your pool account (e.g., Ethermine, SupportXMR) to track your earnings and payouts.

Step 3: Troubleshooting Common Issues

3.1 Miner Not Working

- **Check Your Internet Connection**: Ensure your device is connected to the internet.

- **Verify Your Wallet Address**: Double-check that you've entered the correct wallet address in your mining software or pool settings.

- **Update Your Software**: Make sure you're using the latest version of your mining software.

3.2 Low Hash Rate

- **Check Your Hardware**: Ensure your hardware is properly connected and configured.

- **Adjust Cooling**: Overheating can reduce performance. Use cooling pads for laptops or additional fans for mining rigs.

- **Update Drivers**: Make sure your GPU drivers are up to date.

3.3 High Rejection Rate

- **Check Your Internet Latency**: A slow or unstable internet connection can cause rejected shares. Try connecting to a pool server closer to your location.

- **Adjust Mining Intensity**: Some mining software allows you to adjust the intensity of your mining. Lowering the intensity can reduce rejected shares.

Step 4: Calculating Your Profits

4.1 Understanding Mining Profitability

Mining profitability depends on several factors:

- **Hash Rate**: The higher your hash rate, the more you'll earn.

- **Electricity Costs**: Mining consumes a lot of electricity, so your profits depend on your electricity rates.

- **Cryptocurrency Price**: The value of the cryptocurrency you're mining can fluctuate, affecting your earnings.

4.2 Using Online Calculators

Online mining profitability calculators can help you estimate your earnings. Here's how to use one:

1. Go to a mining calculator like WhatToMine or CryptoCompare.

2. Enter your hardware details (e.g., GPU model, hash rate).

3. Enter your electricity costs (in $/kWh).

4. The calculator will estimate your daily, weekly, and monthly earnings.

4.3 Example Calculation

Let's say you're mining Ethereum with a single NVIDIA GTX 1660 GPU:

- **Hash Rate**: 25 MH/s

- **Electricity Cost**: $0.10/kWh

- **Power Consumption**: 120W

- **Ethereum Price**: $1,500

Using a mining calculator, you might find that you'll earn around **$1.50 per day** after accounting for electricity costs.

Step 5: Scaling Up Your Mining Operation

5.1 When to Scale Up

- **Consistent Earnings**: If you're earning a steady profit, consider investing in more hardware.

- **Market Trends**: If the price of the cryptocurrency you're mining is rising, it might be a good time to expand.

5.2 How to Scale Up

- **Add More GPUs**: If you're using a mining rig, you can add more GPUs to increase your hash rate.

- **Upgrade Hardware**: Consider upgrading to more powerful GPUs or ASIC miners.

- **Diversify**: Mine multiple cryptocurrencies to spread your risk.

Key Takeaways from Chapter 5

- Start your mining operation by launching your mining software and entering your wallet address.

- Monitor key metrics like hash rate, accepted shares, temperature, and earnings.

- Troubleshoot common issues like low hash rate, high rejection rate, and miner not working.

- Use online calculators to estimate your profits based on your hardware and electricity costs.

- Scale up your mining operation by adding more hardware or upgrading your equipment.

Next Chapter Preview: Chapter 6 – Staying Updated and Future

In the next chapter, we'll explore how to stay updated with the latest trends in cryptocurrency mining. You'll learn about the impact of new technologies like Ethereum 2.0, emerging cryptocurrencies, and the role of renewable energy in mining. We'll also discuss regulations and legal considerations.

Start your Cryptocurrency Mining in just 6 hours

.

Start your Cryptocurrency Mining in just 6 hours

CHAPTER 6 – SIX HOUR
STAYING UPDATED AND FUTURE TRENDS

Cryptocurrency **mining is a dynamic** and ever-evolving field. **To stay profitable** and competitive, it's essential to **keep up with the latest trends, technologies, and regulations**. In this chapter, we'll explore how to stay informed, discuss emerging trends in mining, and look at the future of cryptocurrency mining. By the end of this chapter, you'll have the tools and knowledge to adapt to changes in the crypto world.

Step 1: Keeping Up with the Cryptocurrency World

1.1 Follow News and Updates

Staying informed is key to success in cryptocurrency mining. Here's how to keep up with the latest news:

- **Crypto News Websites**:

  - Visit websites like CoinDesk, Cointelegraph, and CryptoSlate for daily updates.

- **Social Media**:

  - Follow influential figures and organizations on Twitter, Reddit, and LinkedIn.

  - Join crypto-related subreddits like r/CryptoCurrency and r/BitcoinMining.

- **YouTube Channels**:

  - Subscribe to channels like **Coin Bureau** for in-depth analysis and tutorials.

1.2 Join Online Communities

Online communities are a great way to connect with other miners, share tips, and stay updated. Here are some popular options:

- **Forums**:

  - Join forums like BitcoinTalk and Crypto Mining Talk.

- **Discord and Telegram Groups**:

  - Many mining pools and crypto projects have active Discord or Telegram communities.

- **Local Meetups**:

  - Check platforms like Meetup.com for local cryptocurrency and mining groups.

Step 2: Future Trends in Cryptocurrency Mining

2.1 The Impact of Ethereum 2.0

- **What is Ethereum 2.0?**:
  Ethereum 2.0 is an upgrade to the Ethereum network that shifts from **Proof of Work (PoW)** to **Proof of Stake (PoS)**.

- **Impact on Miners**:

  - PoS eliminates the need for mining, which means GPU miners will no longer be able to mine Ethereum.

  - Miners may need to switch to other coins like Ravencoin or Ethereum Classic.

2.2 Emerging Cryptocurrencies

New cryptocurrencies are constantly being developed, and some may offer profitable mining opportunities. Here are a few to watch:

- **Ravencoin (RVN)**: Designed for asset transfers, Ravencoin is GPU-friendly and popular among miners.

- **Ergo (ERG)**: A decentralized blockchain with a focus on mining fairness and efficiency.

- **Flux (FLUX)**: A scalable blockchain that supports decentralized computing and GPU mining.

2.3 The Role of Renewable Energy

- **Why It Matters**:
  Mining consumes a significant amount of electricity, and renewable energy can reduce costs and environmental impact.

- **How to Get Started**:

- o Consider using solar panels or wind turbines to power your mining operation.

- o Look for mining pools that use renewable energy, like **Solar-Powered Mining Pools**.

Step 3: Regulations and Legal Considerations

3.1 Understanding the Legal Landscape

Cryptocurrency mining is subject to regulations that vary by country and region. Here's what you need to know:

- **Tax Implications**:

  - o Mining earnings are often considered taxable income. Keep detailed records of your earnings and expenses.

  - o Consult a tax professional to ensure compliance with local laws.

- **Energy Regulations**:

  - o Some regions have restrictions on energy usage for mining. Check local regulations before setting up a large mining operation.

- **Licensing Requirements**:

  - o In some countries, miners may need a license or permit to operate legally.

3.2 Staying Compliant

- **Keep Records**: Maintain detailed records of your mining activities, including earnings, expenses, and hardware purchases.

- **Consult Professionals**: Work with a lawyer or accountant who specializes in cryptocurrency to ensure compliance.

- **Stay Informed**: Regularly check for updates to local and international regulations.

Step 4: Adapting to Changes

4.1 Diversifying Your Mining Portfolio

- **Why It's Important**:
  Diversifying reduces risk and ensures you're not reliant on a single cryptocurrency.

- **How to Diversify**:

  o Mine multiple cryptocurrencies (e.g., Bitcoin, Ethereum, and Ravencoin).

  o Invest in different types of hardware (e.g., GPUs and ASICs).

4.2 Upgrading Your Hardware

- **When to Upgrade**:

  o If your hardware is outdated or no longer profitable, consider upgrading to newer models.

- **What to Look For**:

  o Higher hash rates, lower power consumption, and compatibility with multiple coins.

4.3 Exploring Alternative Mining Methods

- **Cloud Mining**:

  o Rent mining power from a remote data center.

  o Pros: No hardware required, easy to get started.

- o   Cons: Lower profitability, risk of scams.

- **Staking**:

  - o   Earn rewards by holding and "staking" certain cryptocurrencies (e.g., Ethereum 2.0, Cardano).

  - o   Pros: Energy-efficient, no hardware required.

  - o   Cons: Requires a significant upfront investment in coins.

Next Chapter Preview: Chapter 7 – Bonus Tips and Resources

- Stay informed by following crypto news websites, social media, and online communities.

- Keep an eye on emerging trends like Ethereum 2.0, new cryptocurrencies, and renewable energy.

- Understand and comply with local regulations to avoid legal issues.

- Adapt to changes by diversifying your mining portfolio, upgrading your hardware, and exploring alternative mining methods.

Start your Cryptocurrency Mining in just 6 hours

.

Start your Cryptocurrency Mining in just 6 hours

CHAPTER 7 -

Chapter 7: Bonus Tips and Resources

Congratulations! You've made it to the final chapter of this eBook. By now, you've learned how to set up your wallet, choose mining hardware, install mining software, and start your mining operation. In this chapter, we'll share **bonus tips** to maximize your mining efficiency, recommend **tools and resources** for further learning, and highlight **common mistakes to avoid**. We'll also provide a **glossary of key terms** and a list of **recommended hardware and software**.

Bonus Tips for Maximizing Mining Efficiency

1. Reduce Electricity Costs

Electricity is one of the biggest expenses in mining. Here's how to save:

- **Use Renewable Energy**: Consider solar panels or wind turbines to power your mining operation.

- **Optimize Power Settings**: Adjust your hardware's power settings to reduce consumption without sacrificing performance.

- **Take Advantage of Off-Peak Rates**: Mine during off-peak hours when electricity rates are lower.

2. Optimize Cooling

Overheating can damage your hardware and reduce efficiency. Here's how to keep your equipment cool:

- **Use Cooling Pads**: For laptops, use cooling pads to improve airflow.

- **Install Additional Fans**: For mining rigs, add extra fans or use an open-air frame.

- **Monitor Temperatures**: Use software like **HWMonitor** or **MSI Afterburner** to track your hardware's temperature.

3. Overclocking and Undervolting

- **Overclocking**: Increase your hardware's clock speed to boost hash rates. Be cautious, as this can increase power consumption and heat.

- **Undervolting**: Reduce your hardware's voltage to lower power consumption and heat without significantly affecting performance.

4. Join a Mining Pool

Mining pools increase your chances of earning rewards by combining your hash power with other miners. Choose a pool with low fees and a good reputation.

Recommended Resources

1. Books

- **"Mastering Bitcoin" by Andreas M. Antonopoulos**: A comprehensive guide to Bitcoin and blockchain technology.

- **"The Internet of Money" by Andreas M. Antonopoulos**: Explains the broader implications of cryptocurrency.

2. Websites

- **WhatToMine**: A mining profitability calculator.

- **CoinMarketCap**: Tracks cryptocurrency prices and market trends.

- **CryptoCompare**: Provides tools and data for miners and traders.

3. Tools and Software

- **HWMonitor**: Monitors your hardware's temperature and performance.

- **MSI Afterburner**: Allows you to overclock and undervolt your GPU.

- **NiceHash**: A beginner-friendly mining software that automatically selects the most profitable coin to mine.

4. Common Mistakes to Avoid

1. Overinvesting in Hardware

- **Why It's a Problem**: Mining hardware can be expensive, and prices can drop quickly.

- **How to Avoid It**: Start small and scale up as you gain experience and confidence.

2. Ignoring Security

- **Why It's a Problem**: Cryptocurrency is a prime target for hackers.

- **How to Avoid It**: Use strong passwords, enable two-factor authentication (2FA), and store your recovery phrase offline.

3. Failing to Stay Updated

- **Why It's a Problem**: The crypto world changes rapidly, and outdated knowledge can lead to poor decisions.

- **How to Avoid It**: Regularly follow news, join online communities, and stay informed about new trends and technologies.

Glossary of Key Terms

- **Blockchain**: A decentralized digital ledger that records transactions.

- **Hash Rate**: The speed at which your hardware can solve mining problems.

- **Mining Pool**: A group of miners who combine their hash power to increase their chances of earning rewards.

- **Private Key**: A cryptographic code that gives you access to your cryptocurrency.

- **Proof of Work (PoW)**: A consensus mechanism that requires miners to solve complex problems to validate transactions.

- **Proof of Stake (PoS)**: A consensus mechanism that selects validators based on the number of coins they hold and are willing to "stake."

Recommended Hardware and Software

Hardware

- **Mini-Miners**: NerdMiner V2 Pro, Antminer U3.

- **GPUs**: NVIDIA GTX 1660, AMD RX 580.

- **ASICs**: Antminer S19, Whatsminer M30S.

Software

- **Mining Software**: XMRig, PhoenixMiner, CGMiner.

- **Wallets**: Exodus, Ledger Nano X, Trezor.

- **Monitoring Tools**: HWMonitor, MSI Afterburner.

Final Words of Advice

Cryptocurrency mining is an exciting and potentially profitable venture, but it requires patience, persistence, and a willingness to learn. Start small, stay informed, and always prioritize security. As you gain experience, you'll be able to optimize your mining operation and maximize your earnings.

Remember, the crypto world is constantly evolving, so stay curious and keep learning. Good luck, and happy mining!

Appendices

- **Appendix A**: Glossary of Cryptocurrency Terms

- **Appendix B**: Recommended Hardware and Software List

- **Appendix C**: Useful Online Calculators

APPENDIX A
Expanded Glossary of Cryptocurrency Terms

Here's a more comprehensive glossary of cryptocurrency and mining-related terms to help you navigate the world of crypto with confidence:

A

- **Altcoin**: Any cryptocurrency other than Bitcoin (e.g., Ethereum, Litecoin, Dogecoin).

- **ASIC (Application-Specific Integrated Circuit)**: A specialized hardware device designed for mining specific cryptocurrencies.

B

- **Block**: A group of transactions recorded on the blockchain.

- **Block Reward**: The cryptocurrency reward given to miners for successfully adding a block to the blockchain.

- **Blockchain**: A decentralized digital ledger that records transactions across a network of computers.

C

- **Cold Wallet**: A cryptocurrency wallet that is not connected to the internet, providing enhanced security (e.g., hardware wallets, paper wallets).

- **Consensus Mechanism**: A method used by blockchain networks to agree on the validity of transactions (e.g., Proof of Work, Proof of Stake).

- **Cryptocurrency**: A digital or virtual currency that uses cryptography for security.

D

- **Decentralization**: The distribution of control and decision-making across a network, rather than being centralized in a single entity.

- **Difficulty**: A measure of how hard it is to solve the cryptographic puzzle required to mine a block.

E

- **Exchange**: A platform where you can buy, sell, or trade cryptocurrencies (e.g., Binance, Coinbase).

- **Ethereum**: A decentralized blockchain platform that supports smart contracts and decentralized applications (dApps).

F

- **Fiat Currency**: Traditional government-issued currency (e.g., USD, EUR).

- **Fork**: A split in a blockchain, resulting in two separate versions (e.g., Bitcoin and Bitcoin Cash).

G

- **GPU (Graphics Processing Unit)**: A type of hardware used for mining cryptocurrencies, especially those that are GPU-friendly (e.g., Ethereum).

- **Gas Fee**: A fee paid to process transactions on the Ethereum network.

H

- **Hash Rate**: The speed at which a mining device can solve cryptographic problems, measured in hashes per second (H/s).

- **Hot Wallet**: A cryptocurrency wallet connected to the internet, making it convenient but less secure than cold wallets.

I

- **ICO (Initial Coin Offering)**: A fundraising method where new cryptocurrencies are sold to investors before being listed on exchanges.

- **Immutable**: A characteristic of blockchain technology where data, once recorded, cannot be altered.

K

- **Key Pair**: A set of cryptographic keys consisting of a public key (used to receive funds) and a private key (used to access and send funds).

L

- **Ledger**: A record of financial transactions, often referring to the blockchain in cryptocurrency.

- **Liquidity**: The ease with which a cryptocurrency can be bought or sold without affecting its price.

M

- **Mining**: The process of validating transactions and adding them to the blockchain in exchange for rewards.

- **Mining Pool**: A group of miners who combine their computing power to increase their chances of earning rewards.

N

- **Node**: A computer connected to a blockchain network that validates and relays transactions.

- **Nonce**: A number used in mining to solve the cryptographic puzzle and create a new block.

P

- **Private Key**: A cryptographic code that allows you to access and manage your cryptocurrency.

- **Proof of Stake (PoS)**: A consensus mechanism where validators are chosen based on the number of coins they hold and are willing to "stake."

- **Proof of Work (PoW)**: A consensus mechanism that requires miners to solve complex mathematical problems to validate transactions.

R

- **Rejection Rate**: The percentage of shares submitted by a miner that are rejected by the mining pool.

- **Rig**: A setup of hardware (e.g., GPUs, ASICs) used for mining cryptocurrency.

S

- **Satoshi**: The smallest unit of Bitcoin, named after its creator, Satoshi Nakamoto (1 Bitcoin = 100,000,000 Satoshis).

- **Smart Contract**: A self-executing contract with the terms of the agreement directly written into code (e.g., on Ethereum).

- **Staking**: The process of holding and "staking" cryptocurrency to support a blockchain network and earn rewards.

T

- **Transaction Fee**: A fee paid to miners or validators for processing a transaction on the blockchain.

- **Token**: A digital asset built on an existing blockchain (e.g., ERC-20 tokens on Ethereum).

W

- **Wallet**: A tool that stores your private keys and allows you to send, receive, and manage your cryptocurrency.

- **Whale**: An individual or entity that holds a large amount of cryptocurrency, capable of influencing market prices.

Z

- **Zero Confirmation Transaction**: A transaction that has been broadcast to the network but not yet confirmed by miners.

Why This Glossary Matters

Understanding these terms will help you navigate the cryptocurrency and mining world with confidence. Whether you're reading news, joining discussions, or setting up your mining operation, this glossary will serve as a handy reference.

.

APPENDIX B
RECOMMENDED HARDWARE AND SOFTWARE LIST

To help you get started with cryptocurrency mining, here's a detailed list of **recommended hardware and software**. These tools are beginner-friendly, widely used, and have proven to be effective for mining various cryptocurrencies.

Hardware Recommendations

1. Mini-Miners (Beginner-Friendly)

Mini-miners are small, affordable devices perfect for beginners who want to dip their toes into mining without a large upfront investment.

- **NerdMiner V2 Pro:**

    o **Hash Rate**: 78 KH/s (Bitcoin mining).

    o **Power Consumption**: Low (USB-powered).

    o **Best For**: Learning and small-scale Bitcoin mining.

- **Antminer U3:**

    o **Hash Rate**: 63 GH/s (Bitcoin mining).

    o **Power Consumption**: 60W.

    o **Best For**: Affordable Bitcoin mining.

2. GPUs (Graphics Processing Units)

GPUs are versatile and can mine a variety of cryptocurrencies, making them a popular choice for beginners and experienced miners alike.

- **NVIDIA GTX 1660**:

    o **Hash Rate**: ~25 MH/s (Ethereum).

    o **Power Consumption**: 120W.

    o **Best For**: Ethereum and other GPU-mineable coins.

- **AMD RX 580**:

    o **Hash Rate**: ~30 MH/s (Ethereum).

    o **Power Consumption**: 185W.

    o **Best For**: Ethereum and other GPU-mineable coins.

3. ASICs (Application-Specific Integrated Circuits)

ASICs are specialized devices designed for mining specific cryptocurrencies. They are highly efficient but less versatile than GPUs.

- **Antminer S19 Pro**:

    o **Hash Rate**: 110 TH/s (Bitcoin).

    o **Power Consumption**: 3250W.

    o **Best For**: Large-scale Bitcoin mining.

- **Whatsminer M30S**:

    o **Hash Rate**: 88 TH/s (Bitcoin).

    o **Power Consumption**: 3344W.

      o **Best For**: Bitcoin mining with high efficiency.

4. Laptops (For Small-Scale Mining)

While not ideal for large-scale mining, laptops can be used for small-scale mining of CPU-friendly coins like Monero.

- **Any Modern Laptop with a Decent CPU**:

  - **Hash Rate**: ~1-2 KH/s (Monero).

  - **Power Consumption**: Varies.

  - **Best For**: Learning and small-scale Monero mining.

Software Recommendations

1. Mining Software

Mining software connects your hardware to the blockchain network and allows you to start mining.

- **XMRig**:

  - **Best For**: CPU mining (e.g., Monero).

  - **Features**: Lightweight, open-source, and easy to configure.

- **PhoenixMiner**:

- o **Best For**: GPU mining (e.g., Ethereum).

- o **Features**: High performance, low developer fee, and easy to configure.

- **CGMiner**:

  - o **Best For**: ASIC mining (e.g., Bitcoin).

  - o **Features**: Open-source, supports multiple cryptocurrencies, and works on Windows, macOS, and Linux.

- **NiceHash**:

  - o **Best For**: Beginners and GPU miners.

  - o **Features**: Automatically selects the most profitable coin to mine and pays you in Bitcoin.

2. Wallets

Wallets are essential for storing, sending, and receiving your mined cryptocurrency.

- **Exodus**:

  - o **Type**: Hot wallet (desktop and mobile).

  - o **Best For**: Beginners and small-scale miners.

- **Ledger Nano X**:

  - o **Type**: Hardware wallet (cold wallet).

  - o **Best For**: Long-term storage and security.

- **Trezor Model T**:

  - o **Type**: Hardware wallet (cold wallet).

- o **Best For**: Long-term storage and security.

3. Monitoring Tools

Monitoring tools help you track your hardware's performance and ensure everything is running smoothly.

- **HWMonitor**:
  - o **Best For**: Monitoring temperature and performance.
- **MSI Afterburner**:
  - o **Best For**: Overclocking and monitoring GPUs.
- **HiveOS**:
  - o **Best For**: Managing and monitoring multiple mining rigs.

Mining Pool Recommendations

Mining pools allow you to combine your hash power with other miners to increase your chances of earning rewards.

- **Ethermine**:
  - o **Best For**: Ethereum mining.
  - o **Fees**: 1%.
- **Slush Pool**:
  - o **Best For**: Bitcoin mining.
  - o **Fees**: 2%.
- **SupportXMR**:
  - o **Best For**: Monero mining.
  - o **Fees**: 0.6%.

Why This List Matters

This list provides a curated selection of hardware and software that is beginner-friendly, reliable, and widely used in the mining community. Whether you're just starting out or looking to scale up your operation, these tools will help you get the job done.

Start your Cryptocurrency Mining in just 6 hours

APPENDIX C
USEFUL ONLINE CALCULATORS

Online calculators are essential tools for cryptocurrency miners. They help you estimate your potential earnings, compare different cryptocurrencies, and determine the profitability of your mining setup. Below is a list of **useful online calculators** that every miner should bookmark.

1. Mining Profitability Calculators

WhatToMine

- **Website**: https://whattomine.com

- **Features**:

    o   Supports a wide range of cryptocurrencies.

    o   Allows you to input your hardware details (e.g., GPU, ASIC) and electricity costs.

    o   Provides detailed profitability estimates, including daily, weekly, and monthly earnings.

- **Best For**: Comparing the profitability of different cryptocurrencies and hardware setups.

CryptoCompare

- **Website**: https://www.cryptocompare.com/mining/calculator

- **Features**:

- o Supports Bitcoin, Ethereum, and other popular cryptocurrencies.

- o Includes options for ASIC and GPU mining.

- o Provides a breakdown of electricity costs and net profits.

- **Best For**: Detailed profitability calculations for specific cryptocurrencies.

NiceHash Profitability Calculator

- **Website**: https://www.nicehash.com/profitability-calculator

- **Features**:

    - o Designed for users of NiceHash mining software.

    - o Estimates earnings based on your hardware and current market conditions.

    - o Displays payouts in Bitcoin.

- **Best For**: Beginners using NiceHash to mine multiple cryptocurrencies.

2. Electricity Cost Calculators

Electricity Cost Calculator by CryptoCompare

- **Website**: https://www.cryptocompare.com/mining/calculator/btc

- **Features**:

    - o Calculates the electricity cost of running your mining hardware.

o   Allows you to input your hardware's power consumption and local electricity rates.

- **Best For**: Understanding how electricity costs impact your mining profitability.

Mining Profitability Calculator by CoinWarz

- **Website**: https://www.coinwarz.com/mining-calculators
- **Features**:

    o   Includes an electricity cost calculator alongside profitability estimates.

    o   Supports a wide range of cryptocurrencies and hardware types.

- **Best For**: Miners who want to factor in electricity costs when calculating profits.

3. Hash Rate Conversion Tools

Unit Converter by CryptoRival

- **Website**: https://www.cryptorival.com/tools/unit-converter
- **Features**:

    o   Converts between different units of hash rate (e.g., KH/s, MH/s, GH/s, TH/s).

    o   Helps you compare the performance of different mining hardware.

- **Best For**: Understanding and comparing hash rates across devices.

4. Break-Even Calculators

Break-Even Calculator by CoinGecko

- **Website**: https://www.coingecko.com/en/calculators/break-even
- **Features**:
    - Calculates how long it will take to break even on your mining hardware investment.
    - Factors in hardware costs, electricity costs, and mining rewards.
- **Best For**: Miners who want to understand the ROI (Return on Investment) of their mining setup.

5. Cloud Mining Profitability Calculators

Cloud Mining Calculator by Minerstat

- **Website**: https://minerstat.com/cloud-mining-calculator
- **Features**:
    - Estimates earnings from cloud mining contracts.
    - Includes options for popular cloud mining providers.
- **Best For**: Miners considering cloud mining as an alternative to traditional mining.

Why These Calculators Matter

These tools are essential for making informed decisions about your mining operation. They help you:

- Estimate your potential earnings.

- Compare the profitability of different cryptocurrencies and hardware setups.

- Factor in electricity costs and other expenses.

- Plan for long-term profitability and ROI.